# Ollie Otter's Special Gift

## A Story From Quiet Pond

Written by Gerald Reminick

Illustrated by Michelle Quintero

Quiet Pond Publications/Palo Alto Books

EL CERRITO

2013

The original manuscript is Copyright © 2011 by Gerald Reminick. This book is copyright © 2013.

Published by Palo Alto Books,
a division of The Glencannon Press
P.O. Box 1428, El Cerrito, CA 94530
Tel. 800-711-8985, Fax. 510-528-3194
www.glencannon.com

First Edition, first printing.

ISBN 978-1-889901-60-2

**Library of Congress Control Number: 2013941778**

All rights reserved. Printed in the United States of America. No part of this book may be used or reproduced, stored in a retrieval system, or transmitted in any form or by any means, electronic, mechanical, photocopying, recording or otherwise in any manner whatsoever without written permission except in the case of brief quotations embodied in critical articles or reviews.

For
Brynn Elizabeth

Once upon a time there was an Otter who lived in a riverbank with his family. His name was Ollie. He loved to play and explore in the river with his friends. Everyone loved Ollie.

One day, Ollie's mother took him aside and said to him, "Ollie, the river here is not large enough for our family. It's time for you to leave and find a new place you can call home."

"But mom," said Ollie, "I don't know where to go and I'm scared that no one will like me. What if they are mean and call me names?"

Ollie's mom replied, "Son, don't worry. You will find a river or pond where you will make many new friends and start your own family." So, Ollie said goodbye to his family and friends and set out on a journey to find a new home.

After travelling many miles, Ollie started to think he would never find a place he could call home. He also began to think he would never swim again.

Then, one day as he was climbing a hill, he came upon Quiet Pond. Ollie was very excited. He looked around and found the pond to be very beautiful and quiet. There was even a small bridge covering a waterfall at one end of the pond.

Ollie began to look for other animals that lived in the pond. He was also very tired from his long journey. He began to yawn and he really wished he could take a little nap.

So, Ollie looked around and found a nice warm spot on the green bank alongside the pond. He lay in the warm sun and before you could count to ten, Ollie was fast asleep. He began to make otter sounds in his dream that sounded like a kitten purring.

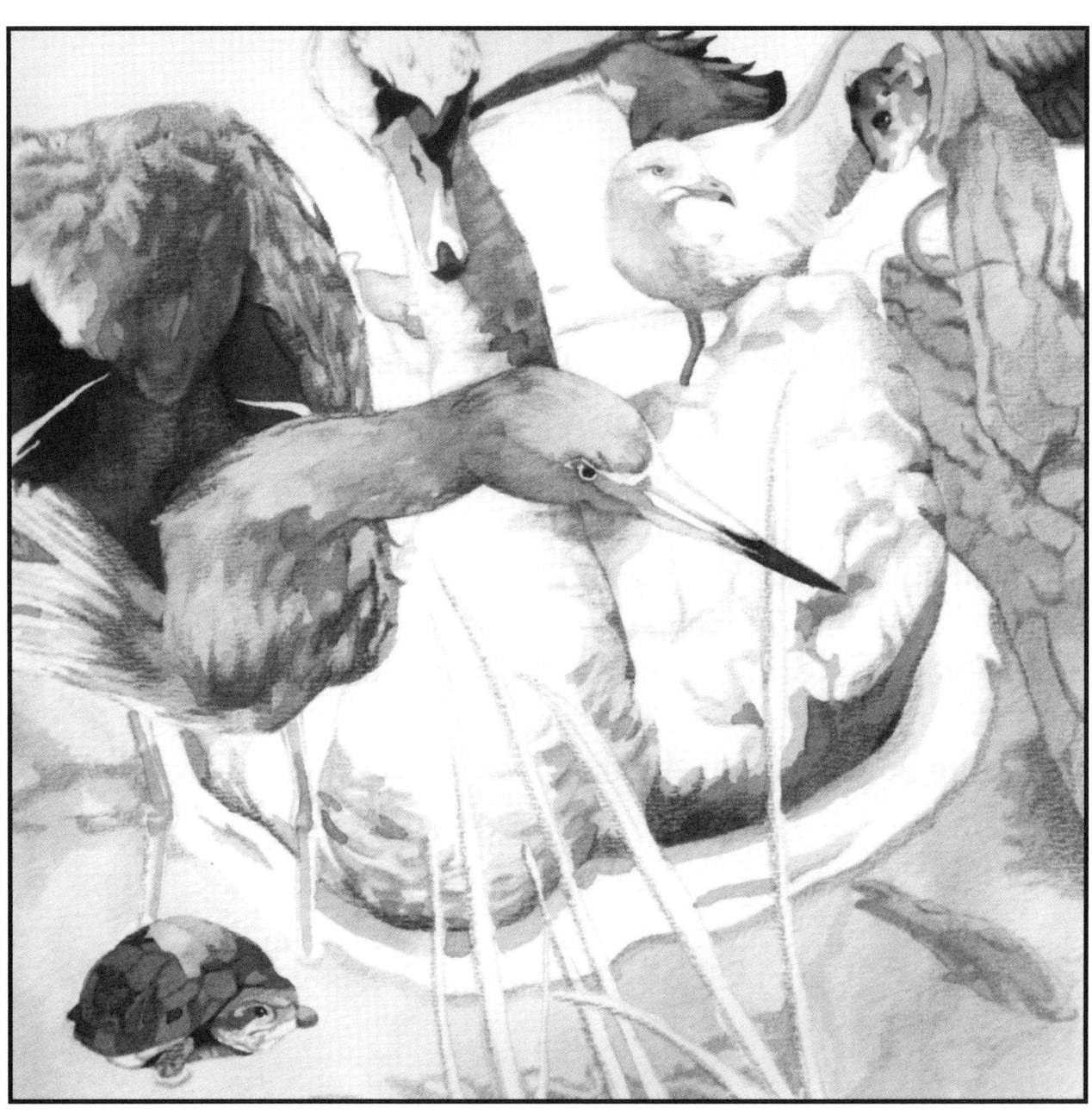

Little did Ollie know that there was a whole group of pond animals watching him from behind a clump of reeds. There was a frog, a heron, a mouse, a seagull, a sunfish, a swan, a trout, a turtle, and others in the group staring at Ollie.

"Just what *is* that sleeping and making all the strange purring sounds?" asked Tom Trout. He whispered to the others in the group to "stay put and I will go and check out the stranger."

Tom hurriedly swam back to the group to tell them that the stranger was indeed different and didn't look like any of them. He had never seen such an animal, and one that made weird purring sounds. After all, this was a quiet place.

None of the occupants were happy to have this noisy stranger sharing Quiet Pond with them.

Many of the animals of Quiet Pond began to move silently toward sleeping Ollie. Sara Swan said, "He's weird looking. He doesn't look like any of us. He doesn't belong here! **Wake him up!**"

So, Tiny Mouse tiptoed over to Ollie and tugged on Ollie's tail and squeaked, "Wake up, wake up."

"That won't do it," said Timothy Turtle who then yelled, **"WAKE UP!"** Ollie began to slowly open his eyes.

Ollie looked around and he was surprised to see so many of the animals of Quiet Pond staring at him.

"Hello," said Ollie. "I'm a river otter."

"**Who cares**," said Blue Heron. "You don't belong here. You are strange looking and you make weird sounds. **Leave now**," he said.

Ollie with a tear in his eye continued, "Please don't make me leave."

Blue Heron then screeched, "**Too bad!** You are not welcome here. Leave our pond at once. You are different than us!"

"I can see that I am different than you but that's all right. You are all friends and neighbors. Just look at yourselves. You all look different too." Ollie then said, "We all have something in common though."

"What do we have in common," asked Sara Swan?

Ollie replied, "Each of us has been given a special gift to help others where we live. I can help you here at Quiet Pond with my special gift."

"**What can you offer**?" asked Tom Trout as he swam around in a circle alongside the bank.

And with that, Ollie bowed before the group and said, "I make others laugh."

All the residents began to shake their heads and wonder. What could he do?

Timothy Turtle said, "**Oh yeah, prove it**!"

Ollie turned toward the group and puffed his chest out and said, **"Just watch me!"** Ollie scampered up to the top of a hill that sloped downward into the pond. What happened next **shocked** the others into silence.

Ollie slid down the hill toward the pond. The group was amazed as Ollie went **swoosh** and with a great **splash** he went **kerplunk** and landed in the pond. The water spray flew outward drenching all of them.

"He's right," the others yelled and they all began to laugh. They shook their heads in amazement and they all began to move toward Ollie.

"Are you alright?" asked Sara Swan.

"You didn't hurt yourself did you?" asked Blue Heron.

Tiny Mouse wiped herself dry from one of the big splashes with a tiny leaf. She couldn't stop giggling over the funny sight of Ollie swooshing down the bank.

Blue Heron went over to Ollie and patted him on his shoulder. "Ollie you are **welcome** to stay here at Quiet Pond. We will gladly help you build a new home."

Ollie beamed a smile and thanked the group.

Sara Swan said, "I'll help you find a hollow in the bank so that you can begin tunneling and building your den."

Ollie was happy to have found a new home in such a beautiful place. The animals all seemed very nice and helpful, now that Ollie had showed them his special gift. Ollie's special gift made them laugh and feel good.

The animals of Quiet Pond began to leave for their homes. They were happy to have such a new and exciting friend at Quiet Pond. They had also learned about the Special Gift.

Ollie Otter

# The End

Good-bye, my friend!